THE VERY FIRST EASTER

Written by
Mary Elizabeth Tebo, FSP
and
Patricia Edward Jablonski, FSP

Illustrated by
Anna Winek-Leliwa

Pauline
BOOKS & MEDIA
Boston

Library of Congress Cataloging-in-Publication Data

Tebo, Mary Elizabeth.
  The very first Easter / written by Mary Elizabeth Tebo and Patricia Edward Jablonski ; illustrated by Anna Winek-Leliwa
        p. cm.
  Summary: Drawing chiefly from the Gospel of Mark, presents the key events surrounding the death and resurrection of Jesus.
    ISBN 0-8198-8032-9 (pbk.)
  1. Jesus Christ—Resurrection—Juvenile literature. 2. Easter—Juvenile literature. [1. Jesus Christ—Resurrection. 2. Easter.] I. Jablonski, Patricia E. II. Winek-Leliwa, Anna, ill. III. Title.
    BT482 .T43 2002
    232.9'7—dc21
                                2001006649

Published in the U.S.A. by Pauline Books & Media, 50 Saint Pauls Avenue, Boston, MA 02130-3491.

Printed in Canada

www. pauline.org

Pauline Books & Media is the publishing house of the Daughters of St. Paul, an international congregation of women religious serving the Church with the communications media.

3 4 5 6 7 8   10 09 08 07 06 05

Jesus is very special. Jesus is God's own Son. Jesus is God because God is his Father. Jesus is human, too, because Mary is his mother.

God our Father sent Jesus to earth. Jesus was born into a Jewish family in a town called Bethlehem. Jesus came to tell us how much God loves us! Jesus also came to save us from our sins (all the wrong things that we do). This is why we call Jesus our Savior.

When Jesus was here on earth, some people were jealous of him. They did not like some of the things he said. They did not like some of the things he did. They got very angry and made Jesus die on a cross. Jesus let them do it. He suffered and died for us because he loves us very much! But this was not the end. Oh, no! Jesus is God. He can do anything! Three days after he died on the cross, Jesus came back to life again! It was the very first Easter.

This is how it all happened….

Jesus went to the big city of Jerusalem. He rode on a little donkey that his friends had borrowed. Many grown-ups and children came to greet Jesus. They shouted, "Hosanna! Blessed is he who comes in the name of the Lord!" Some people cut branches from the palm trees. They waved the branches to welcome Jesus.

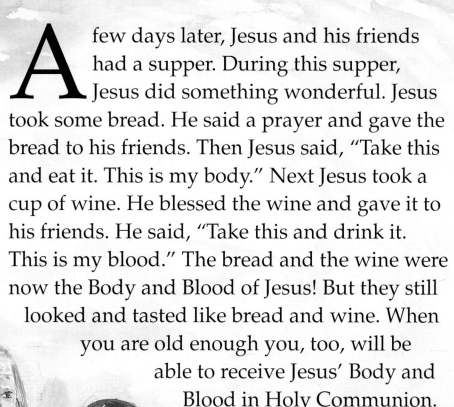

A few days later, Jesus and his friends had a supper. During this supper, Jesus did something wonderful. Jesus took some bread. He said a prayer and gave the bread to his friends. Then Jesus said, "Take this and eat it. This is my body." Next Jesus took a cup of wine. He blessed the wine and gave it to his friends. He said, "Take this and drink it. This is my blood." The bread and the wine were now the Body and Blood of Jesus! But they still looked and tasted like bread and wine. When you are old enough you, too, will be able to receive Jesus' Body and Blood in Holy Communion.

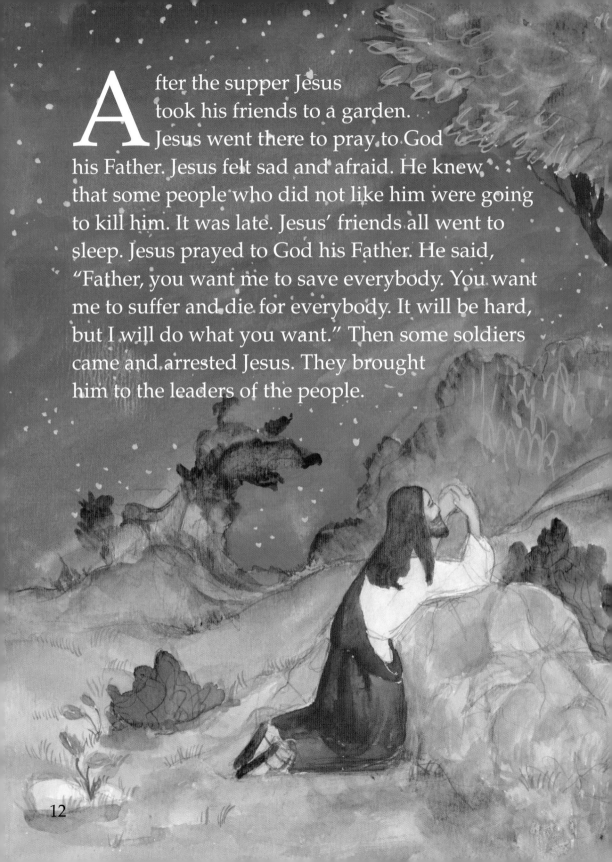

After the supper Jesus took his friends to a garden. Jesus went there to pray to God his Father. Jesus felt sad and afraid. He knew that some people who did not like him were going to kill him. It was late. Jesus' friends all went to sleep. Jesus prayed to God his Father. He said, "Father, you want me to save everybody. You want me to suffer and die for everybody. It will be hard, but I will do what you want." Then some soldiers came and arrested Jesus. They brought him to the leaders of the people.

13

Next, some men told lies about Jesus. The leaders asked Jesus, "Are you really the Savior, the Son of God?"

"Yes, I am," Jesus said. The leaders did not believe Jesus. They were angry. They brought Jesus to Pontius Pilate. Pilate was the Roman governor. He was in charge of the country. At first, Pontius Pilate did not want to kill Jesus. But many people wanted Jesus to die. Pilate was afraid that he might lose his job, so he told the soldiers to crucify Jesus. (*Crucify* means to kill someone on a cross.) The soldiers made Jesus suffer very much. They whipped him. They put a crown of sharp thorns on his head. They made him carry a heavy cross to a hill. Then they nailed him to the cross. Before he died, Jesus forgave everyone who had hurt him. Jesus suffered and died because he loves us!

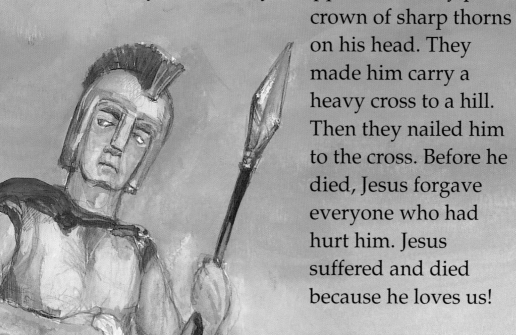

Mary, Jesus' mother, was there when Jesus died. She was so sad! Some of Jesus' friends were there, too. They were so sad! These friends took Jesus' body down from the cross. They carried it to a tomb, which was like a cave. They wanted to wash and take care of Jesus' body the way many people do when someone dies. But it was getting late. So the friends of Jesus rolled a big stone in front of the door of the tomb. Then they went home.

Jesus died on Friday afternoon. Saturday was a holy day for the Jewish people. They could not do any work on that day. Some women who loved Jesus very much wanted to

go back and bury him the right way. They got up very early on Sunday morning. They went to the tomb. They brought special spices to put on Jesus' body. On the way to the tomb, the women said to one another, "Who will roll away the heavy stone for us?" This was a problem. But when the women got to Jesus' tomb they had a surprise! The big, heavy stone was rolled back!

The women went into the tomb. They could not believe what they saw! The body of Jesus was not there. Instead, a young man was sitting inside. He was wearing very bright white clothes. He was an angel. The angel said, "Don't be afraid! You are looking for Jesus, who was nailed to a cross, but he is not here. He is alive again. Go and tell his followers and Peter that Jesus will meet them in Galilee." The women were so afraid. They did not understand what had happened. They ran away as quickly as they could.

After that Jesus himself appeared to one of the women. Her name was Mary Magdalene. Mary Magdalene was filled with joy. It was so wonderful to see Jesus alive again!

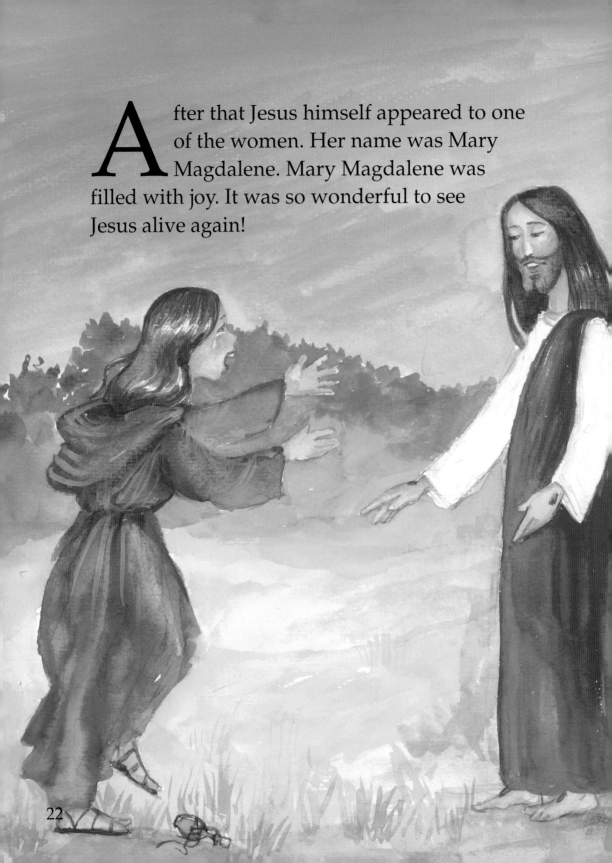

Mary ran to tell the good news to Peter and the other friends of Jesus. These friends were all crying. They were very sad and upset that Jesus had died. They listened to Mary's story, but they did not believe her.

L ater that day, two of Jesus' friends were walking to a town called Emmaus. They were talking about all the sad things that had happened to Jesus. All of a sudden, Jesus came near them. He started walking with them. But they did not know it was Jesus. "What were you just talking about?" Jesus asked.

"We were talking about what happened to Jesus," they said sadly. "He was killed. But this morning some of our friends went to his tomb and they could not find his body."

Then Jesus explained many parts of the Bible that were written about himself.

W hen they got to Emmaus the two friends said to Jesus, "Stay with us for the night!" So Jesus went into the house with them. When they sat down to eat, Jesus took some bread and blessed it. He broke

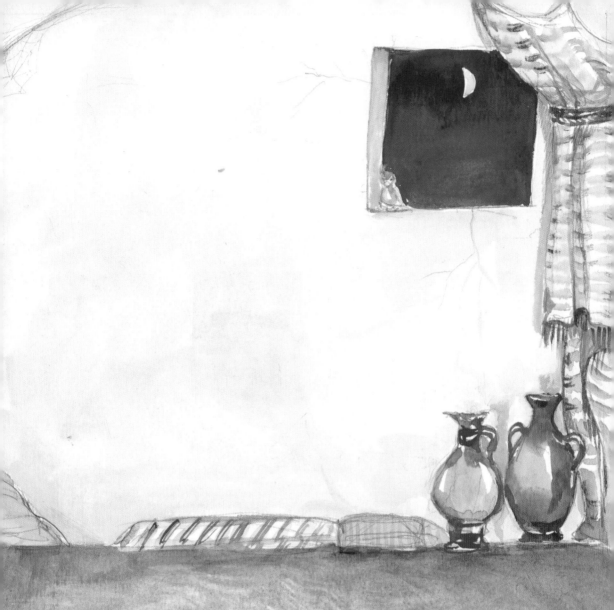

the bread and gave it to them. All of a sudden
the two men knew it was Jesus! Then Jesus
disappeared. The men hurried back to
Jerusalem. They told the other friends of Jesus
what had happened.

Next Jesus went to see his eleven apostles in Jerusalem. The apostles were special friends and followers of Jesus. They were very surprised to see Jesus alive again. They were very, very happy! Jesus told them, "Go and tell everyone in the world about me."

J esus visited his apostles a few more times after he rose from the dead. Then one day he brought them to a mountain. All of a sudden Jesus began to rise up in the air. He was going back to heaven! The apostles watched him go. Then they did just what Jesus had told them to do. They went everywhere to tell people about Jesus. They baptized many people and made them children of God.

If we love God and one another we will live with Jesus in heaven one day. It will be wonderful!

BOOKS & MEDIA

The Daughters of St. Paul operate book and media centers at the following addresses. Visit, call or write the one nearest you today, or find us on the World Wide Web, www.pauline.org

CALIFORNIA
3908 Sepulveda Blvd, Culver City,
CA 90230 310-397-8676

5945 Balboa Avenue, San Diego,
CA 92111 858-565-9181

FLORIDA
145 S.W. 107th Avenue, Miami,
FL 33174 305-559-6715

HAWAII
1143 Bishop Street, Honolulu,
HI 96813 866-521-2731

Neighbor Islands call: 800-259-8463

ILLINOIS
172 North Michigan Avenue, Chicago,
IL 60601 312-346-4228

LOUISIANA
4403 Veterans Memorial Blvd, Metairie,
LA 70006 504-887-7631

MASSACHUSETTS
Rte. 1, 885 Providence Hwy, Dedham,
MA 02026 781-326-5385

MISSOURI
9804 Watson Road, St. Louis,
MO 63126 314-965-3512

NEW JERSEY
561 U.S. Route 1, Wick Plaza,
Edison, NJ 08817 732-572-1200

NEW YORK
150 East 52nd Street, New York,
NY 10022 212-754-1110

OHIO
2105 Ontario Street, Cleveland,
OH 44115 216-621-9427

PENNSYLVANIA
9171-A Roosevelt Blvd, Philadelphia,
PA 19114 215-676-9494

SOUTH CAROLINA
243 King Street, Charleston,
SC 29401 843-577-0175

TENNESSEE
4811 Poplar Avenue, Memphis,
TN 38117 901-761-2987

TEXAS
114 Main Plaza, San Antonio,
TX 78205 210-224-8101

VIRGINIA
1025 King Street, Alexandria,
VA 22314 703-549-3806

CANADA
3022 Dufferin Street, Toronto,
Ontario, Canada M6B 3T5
416-781-9131

¡También somos su fuente para libros, videos y música en español!